Foreword by **Rev. Patrick Otieku-Boadu**
General Secretary, Victory Bible Church International

CHEAT ON
FEAR

Richard Akita

Cheat on FEAR
Copyright © 2015 by Richard Akita

Ordering Information:
Quantity sales. Special discounts are available on quantity
purchases by corporations, churches, schools, associations and
others. For details, contact the publisher at the address above,
Email or call.
E-mail: info@richardakita.com
Call: 0263 260 101

Printed by Launchpad Press
First Printing, 2015

ISBN: 978-9988-2-2633-6

Designed by:
Indes Procom Ltd.
+233(0)26 488 1018

Editing by:
Spearhead Consult
+233(0)20 650 0004

CONTENTS

CHAPTERS   PAGES

Dedication .... *iv*
Acknowledgements .... *v*
Foreword .... *vii*
Introduction .... *ix*
Prologue .... *ix*

1. Definition of Fear 1
2. Paralysis by Analysis 13
3. Remarkable businesses that were launched from garages 25
4. You failed so what? 31
5. Attitude Matters 41
6. Harnessing the energy fear gives 51
7. Use the Fear 59
8. Small Steps, Big Change 75
9. Conclusion 85

Epilogue *94*
References *97*

DEDICATION

This is for you, Najate, your constant love, encouragement, coaching and unfailing believe in my vision has spurred me on to overcome one of my greatest internal conflict.

To my children Marcelle and Ryzard, for looking up to me and keeping my focus on the benefit to teaching both of you the lessons of being free of fear.

And for all who have overcome fear, tamed fear or may still be within grasp of victory, be encouraged for fear is only defeated through renewing your mind.

I cheated on fear and therefore, YOU CAN!

ACKNOWLEDGEMENT

*For all that I am thank
you Lord
For all that I achieve and
become thank you Lord
For being my rock and
foundation thank you Lord*

Who but you alone are able to do exceedingly, abundantly far above all my thoughts and prayers, teaching me through life lessons so that I can continue to be a light to my sphere of influence, through your power that works in me.

A big thank you to Rev. Tony Peters and Rev. Shola Peters, thank you for giving me the guidance, support, teaching and mentoring. Your efforts has been key to my victory. God bless you both and The King's House family.

A big thank you to Marcelle Akita for proofreading the drafts, your patience is awesomely appreciated.

FOREWORD

Fear has, indeed, stopped many dreams than can be imagined. The fear of pain, the fear of failure, the fear of the unknown, the fear of shame, the fear of starting something novel, the fear of rejection and the fear of death have immobilised literally millions of people from gravitating towards their dreams and aspirations.

The approach we are advised by Richard Akita to adapt is that of confrontation. We are admonished to confront our fears despite the seemingly humongous repercussions because Richard says that fear is an illusion with real and tangible effects.

For us to conquer fear, one must develop the toughness of his/her mindset by inflating it with the requisite knowledge to be able to deflate the grips of fear and its lingering emotional torture.

A good posture is for fear to be used as a catalyst for movement towards one's aspirations and not for fear to render us as a monument just for a historical commentary value.

Richard says fear can be cheated on and disarmed so that your mission and vision will be realised not only in our lifetime but centuries after our departure. I wish all who read this book very well. Stay blessed and enjoy.

Rev. Patrick Otieku-Boadu
General Secretary
Victory Bible Church International

INTRODUCTION

Fear: *False Evidence Appearing Real* - that's what I've known fear to be forever. But after reading the manuscript of Cheat on Fear, I've changed my heart. I have used the phrase change of heart intentionally because fear is an emotion that resides in the heart. The mind has a role, but it really grips the heart. *False Evidence Appearing Real* isn't wholly untrue, it's just not totally true either. Evidence that leads to fear is concrete, it is real.

I live in Ghana and I know the statistics of failure in business, failure in academia or relationships or career. These are real, hard facts, not false evidence. Fear is real and it has a crippling effect. It has the power to prevent you from doing anything - the fear of repeated failure (with a past experience), the fear of embarrassment if your attempt flops or just the fear of the unknown.

This book suggests a basic yet phenomenal change in our approach to fear: face your fear by acting in the direction of your fear. Don't run away from it, run to it.

Too many times we short-change ourselves and settle for less than our full potential because we're afraid. "What will they say if I fail?" can be the thought that prevents you from taking a step in the direction of your dreams. What about thinking 'what if I succeed?' For young people experimenting with business ideas or career paths or pursuing their purpose, fear can be the factor that keeps you small, unknown and unfulfilled. Face it.

Richard has focused on what fear really is and how attack it. All around us today, there are compelling reasons not to attempt, reasons not to try, not to risk. Thanks be to God! There are also so many reasons why we must at least try.

I have experienced fear – the fear of not being adequate enough to try something new, not knowing how it will turn out or just being afraid of what will happen if I tried and didn't succeed. Every single time I've faced my fear, I've done well. Whether it's the fear of speaking before a very august audience of young people or before a highly influential audience of business executives, the only way to know if the fear is real, is to face it.

This is a book I recommend to everyone who is second-guessing themselves and wondering if their dream is achievable. I recommend this for everyone pursuing purpose – fear can cripple you, but you can overcome it.

Happy reading.

Petra Aba Asamoah
DipM MCIM, Chartered Marketer

PROLOGUE

'Most people see fear as elite'
— House of Cards

I s this a mirage, an illusion, or the realism of fear that has me encapsulated? Will resisting it or fighting back have any repercussions? Yet, for a moment I dare to contemplate the notion of respite, but even the thought of dealing with fear sends shivers down my spine.

What will the freedom of fear feel or look like?

Can I ever free myself from its tightening grip and dominance?

How can this be possible when I desire breaking free, but find myself enveloped in the paradox of fear's cyclical nature as it has me swinging like a pendulum to its effects of dependence? Needing a fix to leverage the energy I experience to independence; freeing my thought process, keeps me riveted to the hook.

Is this my indirect high?

Similar to a diamond, life has many spheres which reflect experience(s) and one's perspective is skewed by understanding and perception.

Fear is real and has the propensity to immobilise you, it sneaks in stealthily or teaches you lessons from previous mistakes.

BUT...

I dare to cheat on fear and to leverage opportunities posed as stepping stones, valuable lessons and my vulnerability.

While I acknowledge that this martial attitude to battle fear will be arduously long and, because fear is rooted, I will require persistent resistance during my lifetime, I am resolute that rather than having fear perpetually in mind, a strategy that will continuously work is accosting fear and redirecting my thoughts on the very fear to jolt me into action, which will ultimately create a greater impact on my future. This attitude, based on my perception and experiences, has been the most effective tool in cheating on fear. So guarding my influencers is key.

> *'Use your fear as it makes you stronger'*
> — Richard Akita

01

Definition of Fear

This is the definition of fear by *dictionary. com:*

Fear[1]:

Noun

1. A distressing emotion aroused by impending danger, evil, pain, etc., whether the threat is real or imagined;

the feeling or condition of being afraid.

2. A specific instance of or propensity for such a feeling: an abnormal fear of heights.

3. Concern or anxiety; solicitude: a fear for someone's safety.

4. Reverential awe, especially toward God: the fear of God.

5. Something that causes feelings of dread or apprehension; something a person is afraid of: Cancer is a common fear.

6. Anticipation of the possibility that something unpleasant will occur:

Verb

1. To regard with fear; be afraid of.

2. To have reverential awe of.

3. To consider or anticipate (something unpleasant) with a feeling of dread or alarm:

4. Archaic. To experience fear in (oneself):
I fear me he will ne'er forgive us.

Some people say FEAR[2] is False Evidence Appearing Real.

That's a nice acronym. It's catchy. But is it true?

Calling it False Evidence is saying that fear is an illusion or a lie. However, lies are made of words and fear is an emotion.

We can create fear as a reaction to believing illusions, lies, or false evidence. But fear is not the illusion or false evidence. There is the illusion we imagine in our minds, and then, there is the emotion we create as a natural reaction to that illusion. It's the believing part that makes the illusion

---

[1] *http://dictionary.reference.com/browse/fear*

[2] *Definition of Fear: Published by Gary van Warmerdam April 4, 2010*

APPEAR real – so you could say that we make the illusion appear real.

We can also develop fear as a reaction to something that is real. For instance, if you fly an airplane that suddenly begins to lose altitude and the emergency sign comes on, you are likely to feel fearful. You do not have to panic, but fear is probably going to be there. The evidence is not false. It's real and the fear is too. Evidence is not the same as emotion. Be vigilant in realising that not all fear derives from false evidence, our catchy acronym can be misleading.

Fear is not False Evidence, nor is Fear Evidence Appearing Real. We can create fear as a reaction to false evidence or real experience. Fear is an emotion we create. It is often created as a reaction to things, but with enough awareness it does not have to be.

The phrase about Fear being False Evidence Appearing Real emphasises, at least the fact that we may be reacting to an illusion. The result is that, at best, we are dispelling one illusion in our mind while creating another.

CHEAT ON FEAR!

'Why not intimidate the challenges facing you by turning them into learning opportunities?'
— Richard Akita

I get excited when I think about cheating on fear. This stems from a number of reasons. The first is that I have been victimised by fear for quite a long time. My thought process and decision making were all influenced by something I either feared to do or rather feared not to do. In as much as I dislike saying this, I was almost a captive of fear. Now, I have broken the chains of fear, I am no more a slave.

I have been acquitted, discharged and, if I should boldly state it, this actually means I am liberated from fear-inducing situations or rather charges of fear can no longer be related with me. I am indeed free. This is a book that shares my experience with fear and how it can humiliatingly stagnate the progress of a person. The book also shares insights into how one can muster the courage to also "cheat on fear".

POSITIVE MENTAL ATTITUDE

*'Rich dad required his kids to say,
"How can I afford it?" Instead of
"I can't afford it". The words I can't
afford it shuts down your brain. He
felt the words I can't afford it were
a lie.'*
— Robert Kiyosaki

Your use of certain expressions only justifies the tendencies of functioning fear in your domain(s). Are you likely to be caught repeating, "Oh, this is bad timing, I have to wait some more months or years"; or "I am not sure if this business will succeed, I would rather not venture into it"; how about, "What shows this investment portfolio is viable, it is too risky, better save and keep what I have?"

Are you trapped in anxiety, panic or past failures? Our acceptance of such entrapments is indeed a deception. We stall the progress of our lives in the quagmire of fear.

Has there ever been a time in your life that a demand was placed on you but because of summarised past encounters with failure, you faltered? Then permit me to challenge you into a state where you refuse to live a life of defeat, a life that was lived in the past. Wake up now from the daily doses of accusations you have prescribed and align yourself to the reality of a better mandate.

Why are we faithful to FEAR?

'Inaction breeds doubt and fear.
Action breeds confidence and
courage.
If you want to conquer fear, do not
sit home and think about it.
Go out and get busy.'
— Dale Carnegie

Let us go down memory lane and review by identifying the missed opportunities, unfulfilled goals and failures. Now be honest with yourself and ask why and what were the influencing factors that led to the outcome, whether desired or not.

Here is a personal assessment which will assist you to ascertain the flaws and strengths. So it is imperative to be blunt and critical when answering these questions;

- What happened?

- What was the desired outcome versus the actual outcome?

- What will you do differently when you encounter the same circumstance?

- What action plans do you consider will help you to achieve what you have set yourself to do?

It is easy to apportion blame to situations, circumstances, seasons or people, whenever we fall short of the mark or fail, but when we are honest with ourselves we will come to the realisation that we are the people with the ability to stop, delay and/or hinder our life ambitions.

The life lessons gained by being honest with one's self is twofold;

1. By accepting and taking the responsibility of your actions, you unlock your real success. Success is defined as discovering and living out your purpose.

2. You become better equipped to:

   - address the issues raised,

   - evaluate the outcomes more clearly,

   - initiate corrective actions which will enable you to plan thoroughly,

   - seek the assistance you need; and

   - learn from the failures and change your perspective.

02

Paralysis by Analysis

Fear has a way of subtly affecting our actions without announcing its intentions. For example, you think about doing something, you muster the courage and enthusiasm to research on the topic, product or service. Amazingly all the results confirm and encourage you to make a move, however in the end you somehow fail to implement or launch what you have been thinking about. This may be due to a number of reasons. They may include, embarrassment, the fear of the unknown, the fear of failure, or the fear of success and after some time you may be caught in the trap of inactivity. There is a phrase that comes to mind that may sum up the hesitation we sometimes have that prevents us moving to the next level: "Paralysis by Analysis" or as is commonly referred to as, "Analysis Paralysis".

What do I mean by Paralysis by Analysis? This term simply suggests that by virtue of careful calculations and predictions one ends up making no progress with plans. You have decided not to move on after weighing the options. Paralysis by Analysis is to say that you believed more in the negative predictions than the positive. It suggests that you were easily disposed to an orientation which suggested that your carefully thought out ideas would not work, that the chances of success were very slim, and, as such, you do not want to dare.

Albert Einstein said, *"We are the architect of our future."* This points to our responsibility for the future we are yet to live is a result of the words we have spoken in the past, or simply identify the harvesting of words we speak into every situation. Paralysis by Analysis can also mean you have unintentionally become so overwhelmed with the realisation that to bring your desired idea to fruition requires work, discipline, diligence, commitment and, thus, demands on us. The workload can be seen as mountainous and off-putting. In the midst of this, your response is crucial. Ask yourself, "Do I leverage the adrenaline to pursue or talk myself out of action?

*'The best predictor of future
behaviour is ... past behaviour'*
— Dr Phil

We are creatures of habit, therefore, the impact of historical failures or successes, will sway our pendulum of action. But the strongest resistance to activity is our words.

You are only hurting yourself when you fail to take action or the next steps required. Whatever justifications you make, the onus is on you to face the consequences. If you are waiting for the perfect condition to launch, then you will be disappointed as there is no such thing. There may be favourable circumstances which are rare, but those who boldly take risks will surely encounter opportunities.

I have heard a number of times that it is more risky not to take a risk. This statement is just spot on. I often ask myself why fire fight? In crisis moments, firefighting is necessary, but being proactive affords you the opportunity to plan, put in place contingencies and controls.

> *'Careful evaluation of situations should inform you to dare, to take bold steps to advance forward'*
> — Richard Akita

How can one keep rising and resisting the perpetual cycle of failures with colossal setback?

- Could your faith be the catalyst?

- Can a mentor be the key to unlearning your cyclical habits?

*   Can you ever cheat on fear?

Whilst you ponder on the above questions, is it possible to disobey the strident negative voice screaming out your historical failures and be still enough to hear the silent whisper of encouragement saying, "Yes you can?"

It is time to change your paradigm and build a resistance that will break your faithfulness to fear. Go on it is okay to say, "NO" to fear.

You may not have received many (or any) awards, but, if you believe, you can still share a platform with award-winners, because at one point in their lives, they broke the umbilical cord linking them to the faithful bounds of fear.

As a public speaker I agree with a number of professionals that the fear of speaking is often overcome by speaking. I actually sense we overcome what we fear by doing the very thing we fear. We indeed overcome. We displace that tendency of our predicted response. We move it behind us. We must shake off that limitation, shake off that hindrance, and shake off that challenge.

Let us make it personal. Did I just cheat on fear that has always been my partner because growing up I was shy?

Now any time I get the opportunity to speak, the butterflies in my stomach remind me of limitations of being a shy child. Yet as I mount the podium they fly away. Yes I have once again cheated on fear!

The fear of writing a book is overcome by writing. Get your tablet and start writing, pick your pen, notebook and start writing. As you write, more ideas will flow. You will recollect various ideas that are in sync with what you are writing. Can I suggest something to you? Write that book!

The fear of starting a business is crippled by starting it. You start to cheat on fear when you take the step to write down the business plan, include practical ways of raising funds, projecting the sustainability of the business a decade ahead and even the opportunities for it to be trans-generational. Oh, your company can even be a global company.

Did you know that Coca-Cola started from a chemist shop? Do you want to know about the Central University College? It is said that it commenced from a garage.

A garage is unusual, but the very action of starting small does not hinder the potential of amazing growth. Could your greatness be trapped in your inability to see amazing things from your garage? Needless to say that it is not where you start from, but rather, the commencement, consistency, diligence and commitment all rolled into one word, "PASSION," which determines your level of success.

A good friend of mine, Dr Kevin Storr, Prairie View A&M University, USA, illustrates that the a seed's potential is that of a forest[3];

'The potential of Seed is a forest'

First the fruit you enjoy for a few minutes provides nourishment yet has the potential to provide more than you can imagine.
Sadly, whenever we finish eating a fruit we discard the seeds. Why?

---

[3] *Dr Kevin Storr, Houston – Fairbanks 1st June 2015*

*Because we miss the creative power
and underestimate the potential
that discarded seed can produce.
It will grow into a tree and produce
more fruit to feed you and your
family.
Those seeds from the fruits when
planted and nurtured will grow
into an orchard and the orchard
when allowed to will grow into a
forest.
Next time you discard a seed just
think of the potential waste.*

It seems a number of great things have been started from garages, sheds, bedrooms and in the boot of cars. With this in mind, you should not give an excuse for lack of premises.

A number of great companies have been started from almost nowhere. There are great technology companies that can trace their roots from garages. I know of fashion houses that started from garages. One key observation I have made in a number of tertiary institutions, particularly in Ghana, is how a business is began and operated from a garage most on the time.

Wait a minute; did you say you cannot start that business? Go out there and get it registered.

03

Remarkable businesses that were launched from garages:

APPLE

Today this company is worth billions of dollars. It amazes most people when they hear the story of the rather humble beginnings of the company, not from anywhere, but a garage. The story is told that in 1972, Steve Wozniack created the first Apple Computer. He later joined forces with the legendary Steve Jobs and another colleague, Ronald Wayne, to launch Apple Computer Company, from the garage of Jobs' adopted parents. It is not surprising that where Steve Jobs grew up is considered historic today because of the impact of his actions.

To disallow fear from stopping you starting means that whatever you may be starting may look small now, but indeed, its future is intentionally bright. You may fail along the way, but that is just feedback on how you can improve, so learn from it, shake it off and move forward.

AMAZON

Four years after Jeff Bezos was named as the youngest Vice President of a successful

Wall Street Investment firm, he decided to pursue a new cause. Jeff started in his garage what is today one of the leading online platforms in book retailing among others. He did not bother himself for a flamboyant office, but his garage. His garage was his office. In fact it was the head office, the main business centre.

The garage was where the ideas were implemented. It was his workshop. Don't you think people could easily have laughed at Mr. Bezos? Well, they most probably did, but Jeff would not allow such thoughts to stagnate a global idea. He decided to cheat on fear.

The story is told that in 1995, Jeff launched Amazon.com from his garage, where he made his first sales. Today, Amazon is a household name. It is arguably the first name that comes to mind when authors think of selling their books globally.

What can you identify as a garage that is symbolic of birthing and venturing out thought out ideas? You can also cheat on fear. You can decide to pursue your dreams despite the discouraging feedback from friends. Honestly, it is simple but hard to follow through, but others have done it. The farmer sees the harvest before breaking fallow ground, the architect sees the finished building before sketching the building, to list a few. Therefore, see the end from the beginning and use that as motivation to keep on working towards the vision. For surely you will sow in famine and reap a great harvest.

Do you really have to worry yourself about failed statistics? Do you really have to consider those who started and failed? Have you ever considered that there is greatness in you to be a pacesetter, to be a role model, to set a record of someone or to have started something new? I see a pioneer in you. I see an inventor in you. I feel strongly that you are an originator. Get up and pursue that dream. Get it started. If you fall seven times you will rise again. There is great joy in knowing this; that you will rise again.

04

You failed so what

People have invested in failed economies and have defied aging economic principles, confounded global statisticians, committed economists and professors, making them go back to their drawing board. There is a new dawn of ideas waiting to be unleashed by one man or woman who is ready to cheat on fear.

One man or woman who is boldly ready to say, "Even if I fail I am not a failure." One person who can say, "Even if I should fail I will learn from that and bounce back." One person who will agree with Scripture and say, "Even if I fall, there is a lifting up for me." There is the dawn of new ideas awaiting one person's readiness to tread narrow roads and to create new paths. Yes the pathfinder, the pacesetter etc. Is it possible that you are the one I speak of?

'No matter how hard the battle gets or no matter how many people DON'T believe in your dream, Never give up!'
— Eric Thomas

The fear of proposing to a lady is indeed overcome by proposing. It starts with a careful introspection to understand one's self. Deep seated prayer for direction and a bold step to tell her she is the one.

One of the qualities most ascribed to the biblical King Solomon is his wisdom. After many years of observation, he concluded, "I have observed something else under the sun. The fastest runner doesn't always win the race, and the strongest warrior doesn't always win the battle. The wise sometimes go hungry, and the skilful are not necessarily wealthy. And those who are educated do not always lead successful lives. It is all decided by chance, by being in the right place at the right time" (Ecclesiastes 9:11).

If you are not prepared to take a chance on your dreams, then you will miss the opportunity to improve yourself, make an impact on the lives of others and contribute to your community. Unfortunately, this pattern of disappointment only strengthens fear. It is amazing how we allow fear to stop us from fulfilling our purpose. Our purpose is our success marker as it gives the satisfaction that cannot be quantified monetarily.

You have to make up your mind not to allow fear to stop you any longer from dreaming dreams and seeing them fulfilled. Maybe, you are one of those people who have a dream, but fear is preventing you from seeing that dream fulfilled. So many of us have done that, we allow fear to cripple us and prevent us from moving forward.

During my confrontation with fear I listened to *Hello Fear* an album by one of my favourite artists, Kirk Franklin. This album was a contributing catalyst in motivating me to cheat on fear. Below is some of the lyrics of the album;

Kirk Franklin[4] - The Story of Fear Lyrics

I can't sing, but I'm gonna work hard for you to like me
Didn't dream 'cuz if I fail then I might be
What they said I was, could I ever say I did it
Tell ya now that I'm second to admit it
Insecure, I can't understand the application
If I applied myself I guess there'd be no situation
But who teaches who when every day's a substitute
I tried to plant love, but it never took root
My soul's got weeds and the roots are too deep
The roots don't sail 'cuz the roots are too deep
Wait

---

[4] *Kirk Franklin: Hello Fear*

ADDC my roots too deep
A kid too afraid to close his eyes and sleep
Can't you hear me stutter every time I speak?
Fear said hello when she left me weak
Love me and left me with abandonment
issues
Pains a secret, but it illuminates in you then
it creates a menu
Put sin on your plate you don't know until
later how much ever you ate
Now I'm watching my weight
Will this album be my best one?
But if it's not y'all on to the next one
So hello fear it's about time we speak
It may take a while 'cause our roots run deep

When we are frustrated to the point of despair, the human resolve dares to take desperate action with the hope that that action will serve notice to fear, instructing it that it is no longer welcome in our lives.

The only way to do so is to face your fear and take action in what you want to do.

This is so true. Many times we have had a dream to do something unique in life, but because of fear we have never taken a step of faith to get started. Many people keep going back to a job that they literally hate. They are fearful of venturing out and starting a business of their own or writing a book, or doing whatever is in their hearts to do. Many die with the dream inside of them.

'The graveyard is the richest place on the surface of the earth because there you will see the books that were not published, ideas that were not harnessed, songs that were not sung and drama pieces that were never acted'
— Myles Munroe

If you have a burning desire on the inside of you to do something with your life, then take some action today. Do not put off any longer, the dream that is inside you. Just imagine living abundantly in wealth, unbridled creativity, bringing a great change for your community, what does that image conjure?

Unfortunately, we become conditioned by our thoughts, actions and the words we focus on. The strongest reminder is past failures or disappointment. These will feed your thoughts the next time you plan to take action. You face a lot of trouble making such decisions, because you are conditioned by your thoughts and shortcomings. You are afraid to take action and face the consequences. You want to somehow look ahead in time to make sure that everything will be perfect.

And you find that;

- You are afraid of failure,
- You want to avoid embarrassment,
- You are just lost.

But you are not alone. There are many like you and I, who find it difficult to decide on one thing and then go for it. Stop overthinking!

> *'Don't let the mistakes and disappointment of the past control and direct your future'*
> — Zig-Ziglar

Everything does not need to and cannot be perfect. Analysis is important, however, at some point you need to stop thinking and take action. Time spent on thinking, researching and planning is not wasted only if it leads to action. Action without direction is harmful.

Attitude Matters

There are two main things you have to cure about yourself to break this problem of analysis paralysis.

1) Overcome the fear of failure:

All you have to do is make an effort and embrace it, learn from it and your aim(s) will get better as you go along.

- You should not get bogged down by what people say about you.

- Limitations are not in your abilities, but in your thinking.

You become your thoughts. So, if you are afraid of failure then your thoughts dwell more on failures than success. By dwelling more on failures you are inadvertently giving more importance to failure and attracting it.

- Change your thinking right now.

- Think yourself as a successful person and accept failure as necessary steps towards success.

2) Change your attitude:

Attitude means "At -It- U-Do"

Bite the bullet and just do it.

- We always regret the time wasted in over-analysis,

- We have a habit of trying to make everything perfect,

- We are always looking for a perfect solution not knowing what perfect means for us,

- What we do not realise is that solution is a noun. It will not work by itself. The key verb is "solve", which requires action.

You have to attempt, make an effort in some endeavour, even if you fail a couple of times. God can turn your efforts and take you into your blessing. It is a learning process. It is a shift of attitude. The only solution is to believe in yourself and

'Just Do It' ~ Nike

God believes in you and says you can do exceedingly abundantly above all you ask or think through the power that works in you.

You might agree with what I say and recognise the problem of paralysis by analysis, but still many of you will not take any action to act. If you want to be successful in life, start early. Make decisions sooner and take action without any fear of failure. Life is nothing, but a series of experiences, the more you experience, the richer you become.

> *'Success is moving from failure to*
> *failure without losing enthusiasm'*
> — Abraham Lincoln

WHO IS HURTING WHEN WE DO NOTHING?

What Is Fear?

Fear is "an unpleasant and often strong emotion caused by anticipation or awareness of danger".

Fear is completely natural and helps people to recognise and respond to dangerous situations and threats. However, healthy fear — or fear which has a protective function — can evolve into unhealthy or pathological fear, which can lead to exaggerated and violent behaviour.

Dr. Ivan Kos lays out several different stages of fear;

- The first is real fear, or fear based on a real situation. If someone or something hurts you, you have a reason to fear it in the future.

- Second is realistic or possible fear. This fear causes a person to avoid a threat in the first place (i.e. waiting to cross a busy road for safety reasons).

- Next, exaggerated or emotional fear deals with an individual "recalling past fears or occurrences and injecting them into a current situation."

The fear which is fuelled by emotion is particularly relevant to conflict. Emotional fear affects the way people handle conflictual situations.

Dealing with Fear by Phil Barker

In a blog by Phil Barker, he addresses the issues of dealing with fear and adds that it is the onus of the individual to deal with fear.

Individuals: There are many ways of approaching fear within the context of conflict. However, since fear is such a personal issue, most approaches focus on the individual. There are various ways to deal with your own fear, including becoming aware of it, identifying the ways you express fear, recognising the situations which trigger fear, and using behavioural techniques to reduce fear and stress.

In order to overcome fear, individuals must first come to terms with their own fears and understand just how destructive they can be. However, it is equally important to be aware of others' fears. Being aware of other people's fear allows you to deal with it appropriately. One of the most effective ways of handling the fear of others is through empathy, or seeing things from the other person's perspective. Once you are able to recognise how your actions could inadvertently be instrumental in causing fear on the other side, half the battle is won. By toning down one's language or clarifying one's interests and needs, it is possible to dispel unwarranted fears, thereby helping the other side feel more secure. Empathy is also important in any attempt at reconciliation or mediation, because it helps to foster a positive interaction between people. It is also important to share your own fears so that others can empathise with you in return, and alter their behaviour in ways that will lessen that fear as well.

In President Franklin Roosevelt's first inaugural address he deals with the issue of fear from a leader's perspective;

> *'We have nothing to fear but fear itself.'*
> — Franklin Roosevelt 1933

"Public support is essential for political leaders. One way leaders can gain this support is by addressing, playing off of, or even causing the fears of his or her people. As a result, leaders can play an important role in the creation and/or calming of fears, particularly in ethnic or inter-group conflicts. It is important that leaders are aware of the consequences of using fear as a motivational tool. Because fear is such a powerful emotion, leaders must be extremely cautious about playing on the fears of people. Former Yugoslavia is a perfect example of how the fears of the people can be used by leaders for power. Serb leaders often played on Serb fears in order to strengthen their power and to push people to do things they might otherwise have refused to do".

Causes of Fear

Conflict is often driven by unfulfilled needs and the fears related to these needs. The most common fear in intractable conflict is the fear of losing one's identity and/or security. Individuals and groups identify themselves by what is peculiar to their social grouping (based on culture, language, race, religion, etc.,) and threats to those identities arouse very real fears; fears of extinction, fears of the future, fears of oppression, etc.

These examples illustrate the important role that history plays in the development of fear. Memories of past injustices lead individuals to anticipate future oppression or violence with a sense of anxiety and dread.

06

Harnessing the energy fear gives

Harnessing the Power of Negativity
Posted on March 6, 2015 by tdadams

Making change is challenging. When
we try to move forward and make
changes in our life we usually reach that

point where we have to push through the discomfort. At this point in the process, we tend to fall back into our comfort zone of familiar feelings. These are the experiences that we know and, while they may not be pleasant, they are familiar and that is why we abandon change over and over.

What is the comfort zone?

The comfort zone relates to five negative feelings:

1. Fear
2. Hurt
3. Anger
4. Guilt
5. Unworthiness

We can, however, use these elements to implement change. First, we must be aware of the emotions we are feeling. Then we must use those emotions to give change momentum.

How can the perceived negative feelings assist us?

Fear Gives Us Focused Energy:

Did you know that sadness is actually anger turned inwards? When we are afraid, our attention is focused, all distractions are eliminated by this intense concentration on what our fear deems as significant, which, ultimately, translates into listlessly acting out what fear dictates. Now imagine if we are to reverse this? Then when we feel fear, we can consciously choose to recognise how its forceful energy can potentially be redirected towards what we are passionate about. We can use this energy to create positive changes in our life.

Hurt can show us where our passion is and how much we care:

When we are passionate about something we often turn to our family and friends for support. When they do not see the vision we see, we hurt and many times lose our dreams. Because others have made us feel as though they were either unimportant or unachievable. We hurt because we care. We care about the idea we have proposed. We can use the energy harnessed from hurt to reconnect with our passion, allowing us to move forward with intention.

Anger creates massive energy for us to use. By assigning ourselves the role as observer, we can be made aware of the deep-seated or surfacing anger, as its harvested energy surges up within. Our heart races, our cheeks flush and our breathing patterns change. As pointed out, that is a power tool that does not need a battery to be productive! We can replace these negative thoughts with positive thoughts *(Law of Substitution)* and remember that what our attention is focused on manifests *(Law of Growth)*.

Guilt is anger directed at self which provides energy for change:

Feeling bad about something which has happened validates that at the core we are good people. These feelings also validate our spiritual compasses, showing that they are working. Mistakes should not be measured as either good or bad, but as opportunities for growth. If what is making you feel guilty can be fixed, then fix it. If not, the past lives in the past, forgive yourself and learn the lesson that presented itself during the experience. Change your beliefs rather than berating yourself. Treat yourself with the same kindness you would show to someone else.

Unworthiness allows us to focus and stay on track:

It is important to be the observer when these emotions surface. Feelings of unworthiness usually surface when we have too much on our plate; when we are overextended. Multi-tasking is not productive, contrary to popular belief, and feeling unworthy reminds us to pull in the reins. We do not have to give anything up, but we do need to prioritize. We need to make a list and work through the list rather than keeping all the balls in the air. Ironically, unworthiness can bring us the most satisfaction, because it reminds us that we cannot be everything to everyone. Remember who you are and what you have to offer and then share those gifts with others.

With this thought in mind, consider preschool children; while busy with activities, they are little sponges, soaking in everything around them. Similar to adults, they too can feel overwhelmed. If you place a toy box in front of a young child, you will usually find that the child digs, and digs, and digs through the items in the box, spilling them onto the floor. The child may eventually find the toy that catches his or her interest, but usually the dissatisfied toddler moves away from the emptied toy box. That is because his or her choices are not clear and what is presented before them requires too much work to make a decision.

If you take that same child and place him or her in a room with toy shelves, where choices are laid out in an organised fashion, he or she will quickly find what they want and begin playing. They may even return to the toy shelf again and again to add other toys to their imaginative play. Their choices are clear and because the feeling of being overwhelmed has been eliminated they are focused and clear on their intent.

The next time we are feeling one of the above emotions, we can remember the nursery school child. Step away from the toy box and focus our energy on our passions. See the comfort zone for what it is and redirect those negative feelings to change momentum.

07

Use the Fear

Fear is defined as, "a distressing emotion aroused by a threat, whether the threat is real or imagined."

As actors, most of our fears are more imagined than actual physical threats, but it does not make them any less debilitating. Eliminating fear indefinitely may be

Cheat on FEAR

impossible; you can learn to utilize it to your advantage. You might not even be aware that it is actually fear you are feeling as it can be disguised as procrastination, doubt, indecision, or even caution.

Let us use a simple phone call as an example. Let us say you want to reach out to an agent for representation. You do not really feel "ready" to make the call, so you go out to Starbucks, find yourself on Facebook, or suddenly notice how badly the house needs cleaning (procrastination). Maybe you wonder if your résumé is strong enough. What if they already have enough of your type? (Doubt). And, - is this really the right agent for you? Perhaps you should do more research (indecision). You finally decide to make the call, but now you are concerned about the time of day. You want to be careful not to annoy the agent by calling when they are busy with the breakdowns (caution). Sound familiar?

Here are some tips on how to use fear so it works for you, not against you.

Connect the feeling of fear with success. Fear is the prelude to potentially great things. Think about any successful moments in your life which were all probably preceded by fear—getting the big promotion, booking the coveted acting gig, landing the agent, etc.,. When you find you are resisting something that you know could be good for your career, then be assured that you are on the right track.

Once you spot fear in any of its forms, work out the worst case scenario in your head. Chances are that if the agent rejects you, you will not lose a limb or die. What is worse than the worst case scenario is no action at all. Make the call, send the email, approach the person, and do not wait.

Time is not your friend. Time will only perpetuate inaction.

Use the physical reaction that fear induces. When we feel fear, even though we are not running for our lives, we still feel a degree of adrenaline — increased heart rate, a tenseness in the muscles, sharpened senses — the exact opposite of being relaxed and comfortable. Now is the time to use the fear induced adrenaline to act.

Be it a phone call, an email, or approaching someone, once you dive in and get into action mode, the outcome is never really as bad as the worst case scenario we have created in our heads. And then, we wonder why we waited so long to do such a simple thing! Practising to control fear with action will begin to make you stronger and more confident in asking for — and getting — what you want to succeed.

Cognitive psychologist, Scott Barry Kaufman, Ph.D., says fear can be a driving force. Often, what you fear in a situation is the possibility of failure. Rather than letting the fear inhibit you, Kaufman says, choose to use it to motivate you toward taking bold steps.

Reprogram Your Fear

Steve Chandler, author of "Fearless: 100 Ways to Motivate Yourself," says many fears are learned reactions, absorbed in childhood from the behaviour of others. Question the origin of your fear. Replace those beliefs with more accurate statements about your capability.

Take Small Steps

Overcome your fear by facing it in small steps. The World Health Organization

Collaborating Centre for Research and Training for Mental Health recommends systematic desensitization, which means exposing yourself to the feared situation in a non-threatening way and slowly facing more challenging tasks. Start by looking at a picture of a snake, for example, then visit the snake house at the zoo, then touch a snake.

Find Your Zone

Anxiety can be countered with mental focus, Kaufman says. Concentrate on the task itself, in spite of your fear. The emotions will fade as your focus creates a state of creative flow.

Get Unstuck

Rumination, the persistent mental focus on negative situations, leads to anxiety, Selby says. Do not allow yourself to dwell on fear. Distract yourself with positive activities. When you think about the fearsome problem, focus on the positive actions you can take rather than negative outcomes.

Rumination is explained as the compulsive focused attention on the symptoms of one's distress. What this means is simply that a person is focusing too much on the negatives or bad instances.

Such people are more oriented towards the negativity and dwell more on what caused it and the effect it has created, without taking action to prevent future occurrence. It is closely related to worry. Whereas worry is often related to the fear of the future, ruminations dig up negative feelings from the past.

The concept of rumination as explained in Psychology is closely related to the term, 'ruminant', which has its roots in the Latin word, 'ruminare', meaning 'to chew again'. To illustrate further, animals like cattle, goats and sheep are classified as ruminants. Ruminants have been identified to have four chambers as part of their digestive system unlike other animals or mammals. Their four-compartment stomach; Rumen, Reticulum, Omasum and Abomasum, have specialised functions, yet they operate together. The concept is observed when the food is chewed and reaches the first two chambers (rumen and reticulum). There they are mixed with saliva and separated into layers of solid and liquid material. Experts say that solids clump together to form what is referred to as the cud or the bolus.

The intriguing thing is that, at this stage, the solid material is sent back to the mouth to be chewed again to allow the solid to be well broken.

Is it well placed, from the description above for one to ask if sometimes   long gone issues, fearful experiences can be brought up to diagnose in minute detail only to let one to remain fearful?

A positive mental attitude should be more preferred as against ruminating. Do not get stuck, cheat on fear. Come, let sleeping dogs lie.

COGNITIVE BEHAVIOURAL THERAPY

Dispel your fear with facts. Cognitive Behavioural Therapy (CBT), a form of Psychotherapy, puts into perspective how behaviours, thoughts and feelings (emotions) are used among other things, to change unhelpful thinking.

The therapy is a union of both Behavioural and Cognitive theories.

The proponents of the behavioural theory are of the view that some behaviours emerge through prior conditioning from the environment and/or from other external stimuli. They are of the view that these behaviours cannot be controlled through rational thought. The theory in itself is described as being 'problem focused' geared towards surging results.

Cognitive therapists on the other hand acknowledge that conscious thoughts could solely influence a person's behaviour.

Eventually the two perspectives were married as the Cognitive Behavioural Therapy.

The approach is effective for a number of conditions, such as, mood, anxiety and psychotic orders. The blend of behavioural and the cognitive school of thought suggest that fear can be dispelled in the face of evidence or facts. They believe that 'distortions' may be caused by a pseudo or false discrimination belief, or rather, an overgeneralization (hyperbole) of something.[5]

Could it be possible that what you are scared of does not really exist or rather you are making a huge fuss unnecessarily?

Psychologists over the years have, therefore, used Cognitive Behavioural Therapy to assist people to be more open-minded and make informed decisions.

---

[5] *This research was taken from the www.cognitivetherapy.com website 21/07/2015*

Fear is often the result of a sense of hopelessness. It is helpful that to move away from fear you focus on your strengths. This concept is closely related to the idea of deliberate positioning. A typical football game observes eleven players in a team during a game. However, we are able to conclude on a player being 'the man of the match'.

PELE

Born in October 1960, Edson Arantes do Nascimento, the Brazilian Portuguese, affectionately known as Pele, is arguably widely regarded as the greatest footballer of all time. Being voted in 1999 by the International Federation of Football History & Statistics (IFFHS) as the World Player of the Century, Pele enviably was in the same year named in the list of '100 most influential people of the 20th Century' by the Time (magazine), the world's largest circulation for a weekly news magazine.

The world's successful people are often known for their strengths. Pele is known for football, playing in a distinct position as a striker.

In fact, it is recorded that his performance in school was not encouraging, but rather abysmal, holding him back on three occasions. Today, however, his name is parallel the heights he attained in soccer and not his academics. I am not speaking against academic excellence I am, however, advocating deliberate positioning and growth in a chosen field of endeavour.

Do not allow your fears to cripple you? Leverage on your strengths. Focus on where you function best. A strategic leverage over fear is a mastery of your chosen field of endeavour. Today we speak of Pele as the greatest footballer of all time, the question is, "Did Pele play in all the eleven positions in football?" Absolutely no! In fact, we almost forget he could not keep a ball, though we generally conclude that he is the greatest footballer of all time.

Your resolve to focus on your strengths or your positive traits will indeed pay off.

GET AN IMAGE

At a stage in my life, I set a number of goals I wanted to achieve for myself. Honestly, some of them were scary. Among them, was my desire to write a number of books that would sell well, to run a clothing line and to give out to orphanages. All of these I wanted to achieve before I turned 50 - and considering them initially was scary – ambition should! To tackle that, I did something significant, I not only wrote down my ideas, but I made pictures of them and pasted them on a board. Gradually, I saw myself achieving my goals. Cheat on fear.

The World Health Organization (WHO) Collaborating for Research Training for Mental Health proposes systematic desensitisation as one of the measures in mental health. They suggest that exposing one's self to a feared situation in a rather non-threatening way can equip the person to gradually face more challenging tasks. What do they mean?

Remember my earlier example of confronting your fear of snakes, here is how WHO describes how that can be achieved.

One can overcome the fear of a rather dangerous animal like a snake by first having an image or picture of the snake in one's room and taking a look at it constantly.

The idea is that as the person does that, the fear of the sight of a snake is overcome. As a further step, it is advised that having overcome the fear of just merely seeing a snake, the person gathers courage to touch the snake on a visit to the zoo. Will you cheat on fear?

08

Small Steps, Big Change

Here are simple steps in overcoming fear[6];

Everyone has fears. Sometimes they serve a rational purpose, such as protecting you from a life-threatening situation. Many

---

[6] *http://www.livestrong.com/article/134351-10-ways-overcome-fear/#ix-zz2GEqBrxGu 21/07/2015*

fears, however, are irrational and prevent people from taking the necessary action to achieving what they truly want. Most people want to overcome their fears, but are not sure about how to do that. Here are some steps that you can immediately implement to help overcome your fears.

1. Be Aware

Dispel your fear with facts. According to the tenets of cognitive-behavioural psychology, fear is often based on inaccurate beliefs. Counter them by listing the facts about the feared situation. Facts allow you to take action, while anxiety prohibits action.

2. Get Positive

Fear is the result of a sense of helplessness. Focus on your strengths as tools against fear. Examine positive skills and traits that have moved you through difficult situations in the past and enlist them in dealing with the present problem.

3. Know Your Own Mind

Fear leads to self-sabotaging behaviour, Selby says, so that we take action to make ourselves feel better in the moment, rather than facing more difficult tasks that will help us reach our long-term goals. Focus on the steps required to reach your goal, rather than procrastinating to avoid your fear of failure.

4. Tend to Mind and Body

Fear produces physiological symptoms that further reduce one's ability to cope with it. Practice meditation and visualisation, breathe deeply, exercise regularly, eat a healthful diet and get adequate sleep to prevent or reduce fear-induced stress.

5.   Scriptures on fear

Meditate, confess and act on God's word

I have selected these scripture readings which were useful to me in my journey of overcoming fear in the hope that you too will find the inspiration to overcome fear. My simple request is for you to make time, read carefully, meditate and speak these scriptures out. Some of you may have come across one or more of these scriptures before but this time, make the scriptures personal.

Speak it out, confess it with your name. For instance, replace 'you' or 'us' with your name.

- **Psalm 23:4:** Even though I walk through the valley of the shadow of death, I will fear no evil, for you are with me; your rod and your staff, they comfort me.

- **Psalm 27:1:** The LORD is my light and my salvation — whom shall I fear? The LORD is the stronghold of my life — of whom shall I be afraid?

- **Psalm 118:6:** The LORD is with me; I will not be afraid. What can man do to me?

- **2 Timothy 1:7:** For God did not give us a spirit of timidity, but a spirit of power, of love and of self-discipline.

- **Psalm 115:11:** You who fear him, trust in the LORD — he is their help and shield.

Psalm 103:17: But from everlasting to everlasting the LORD's love is with those who fear him, and his righteousness with their children's children.

Psalm 112:1: Praise the LORD. Blessed is the man who fears the LORD, who finds great delight in his commands.

Deuteronomy 31:6: Be strong and courageous. Do not be afraid or terrified because of them, for the LORD your God goes with you; he will never leave you nor forsake you."

1 Chronicles 28:20: David also said to Solomon his son, "Be strong and courageous, and do the work. Do not be afraid or discouraged, for the LORD God, my God, is with you.

He will not fail you or forsake you until all the work for the service of the temple of the LORD is finished.

Psalm 56:3-4: When I am afraid, I will trust in you. In God, whose word I praise, in God I trust; I will not be afraid. What can mortal man do to me?

Isaiah 41:10: So do not fear, for I am with you; do not be dismayed, for I am your God. I will strengthen you and help you; I will uphold you with my righteous right hand.

Isaiah 41:13: For I am the LORD, your God, who takes hold of your right hand and says to you, Do not fear; I will help you.

Isaiah 54:4: "Do not be afraid; you will not suffer shame. Do not fear disgrace; you will not be humiliated. You will forget the shame of your youth and remember no more the reproach of your widowhood.

Matthew 10:28: Do not be afraid of those who kill the body but cannot kill the soul. Rather, be afraid of the One who can destroy both soul and body in hell.

Romans 8:15: For you did not receive a spirit that makes you a slave again to fear, but you received the Spirit of sonship. And by him we cry, "Abba, Father."

1 Corinthians 16:13: Be on your guard; stand firm in the faith; be men of courage; be strong.

Hebrews 13:5-6: Keep your lives free from the love of money and be content with what you have, because God has said, "Never will I leave you; never will I forsake you." So we say with confidence, "The Lord is my helper; I will not be afraid. What can man do to me?"

● **1 Peter 3:13-14:** Who is going to harm you if you are eager to do good? But even if you should suffer for what is right, you are blessed. "Do not fear what they fear; do not be frightened."

● **1 John 4:18:** There is no fear in love. But perfect love drives out fear, because fear has to do with punishment. The one who fears is not made perfect in love.

09

Conclusion

Benjamin Franklin said, "Some people die at 25 and aren't buried until 75".

I find this quote apt. When you are young you are full of energy, every new day holds a new discovery, you want to learn everything that you can and as fast as possible, you are full of ideas about how you can change the world – you are alive.

Soon enough you start to grow older, everything becomes a routine, nothing seems interesting anymore; you go to university, you then find a job and now you are 25 years of age waiting for retirement. Without passion for life, without energy, without any plans to change the world, just waiting for retirement and thinking that when you retire you would then experience all the life joys However, you then retire and realise that you do not have energy for anything.

This is the life that the average person is living. Now, I want to ask you a question, do you want a life like that? Do you want to wake up one day and realise that you have not done anything interesting for the last 10 years? Well, I do not and probably neither do you, if you are reading this book.

You do not want to find a job and slave for the rest of your life. Work in a job that you do not even like, wake up early and be stuck in traffic for hours just to get somewhere where you do not want to be and patiently wait for the weekend, the holidays and, of course, retirement.

Would it not be better to live your dream life every day, go on vacations whenever you like, sleep as long as you need and work from home, forget to count what day of the week it is, drive nice cars, live in a beautiful house, have anything you want, and have freedom? It might be even uncomfortable to think about it and you might think you do not deserve it or I should not be greedy or whatever excuse one's mind makes.

Dream big, do not settle for mediocrity! You can do great things, keep learning, keep growing and you will achieve success, whether in your job or building a business, which I highly recommend, because it is the opportunity for a person to have all the freedom, if you set it up correctly.

Life will never give you what you want, but will deliver what you demand, therefore, decide to live and stop surviving.

You have one life decide how you want to live it!

DARE TO DREAM

I dare you, to dream again of the life you envisaged whilst growing up. Back then you spoke about your dreams with passion and defended every facet of it. What happened? Who resisted your dreams with such vigour that it stopped the wind in your sails? Is it possible to dare to dream?

Remember that to cheat on fear you MUST go after your dreams, at least try and when failure comes, use it as a stepping stone and employ its lessons to navigate towards your dream.

I am convinced that the only one that can stop, hinder or abort your dream is YOU.

'No one can stop you but you alone'
— Richard Akita

Life may have beaten you into submission, but you are still alive and recovering your loss is attainable.

During the challenging season, I remember a thought that came to me during a time of prayer; *"As long as you still live, you can recover all"* That thought, for me, interrupted the negativity, hopelessness, despair and spurred me on as I reflected on the huge financial losses I had made from a failing businesses. The impact of the losses and its related induced stress affected my health.

My judgement was impaired and the desire to continue living was a painful reality as I looked at my family and the hurt I had caused, needless to say the loans from banks that needed to be paid back.

While bankruptcy was enticing as a potential solution, the taunting thought of how boastful, confident and prideful I had been in declaring a future of success and living my purpose constantly revived itself. The results were far beyond my expectation I kept reminding myself and resounding the *"I told you so!"* accusation. At that point, death seemed more desirable in ending the cycle of defeat, yet, in my darkest moment the thought *"So far as you still live, you can recover all"*, jolted my attention to the possibility of recovering all. But how was I to achieve that?

I retrained myself to focus on the good lessons, whenever I encountered failure and kept asking myself what I had learnt. I was pushed to seek out its application and apply them. Failure only screams *"not this way"* and sadly because of its potent stridency, we are inclined to give this nauseating scream our full attention. However, there is an inner voice of courage that for the strangest reason only seems to whisper *'try again'*.

In my personal life, I first began to train myself to tune in to that whisper's frequency and that practise assisted me in facing fear head on, because whatever the outcome, I learnt and moved closer to the dream.

Secondly, dealing with the financial quagmire was the biggest giant I had to face. Fear kept reminding me that the banks would reject any form of proposal, but guess what? I did not shy away from speaking to my bankers and this led to them accepting a proposal on repaying the debt.

Thirdly, I spoke to my family on the seriousness of the financial losses and my action plan. I was awe struck by the support of my wife and children, because fear said I would lose my family and they would never forgive me! They are continually my greatest fans, cheerleaders and assets!

Fourthly, I dared to dream again. After a period of soul-searching I realised that my joy stemmed from the passion and drive in training and life performance coaching, which I had been doing unofficially for over 20 years. To monetise it, I retrained and continually developed my skills to operate optimally with my skills.

I cheated on fear and so can you!

Now arise from the fall, dust yourself up, end your pity party, acknowledge your mistakes, take responsibility and forgive yourself for delaying and smile.

Now take a blank sheet of paper and write down the dreams, pause and imagine yourself living the dream. Now ask yourself the route or actions needed to bring the imagined to reality. Write the ideas and seek assistance. Do not worry about the lack of enthusiasm on everyone's part. It is your life and, amazingly, wisdom can be given from your worst critic.

Go on just dare! Dare to Dream.

EPILOGUE

The shadows of yesterday by
— Richard Akita

"A reflection of yesterday that reminds you of the emotional peaks and troughs, moments to savour or spit out.

Yet the power of a memory can be so overwhelming that if you are not careful your reality of pain can flood your mind.

Remember it is the shadows of yesterday.

The shadows of yesterday can influence your today and stunt your tomorrow, only when permitted.

But today has yet to be explored, so why dwell on the "What could haves"?

Remember it is the shadow of yesterday.

The shadows of yesterday may cause us to reminisce, yet they are reference point to be thankful as you experience a new day.

The shadows of yesterday arouse the desire to turn back the clock, yet they give the opportunity to create new memories.

The shadows of yesterday also inform us about His light that shines on us. Our shadow is the tangible evidence.

A lesson you take from yesterday that propels and transforms your outlook so that your reflection no longer haunts you but smiles back and says well done.

Remember it is only the shadows of yesterday.

To live in the present, thrive and metamorphous into the true being you were intended for is to acknowledge the shadows of yesterday and yet press on with the agenda of becoming *YOU.*

Remember the shadows of yesterday are gone; you have today and tomorrow is not guaranteed. Therefore, maximise today by being *YOU.*

REFERENCES

Retta Putignano: Create Your Reel, and Backstage Expert 01/07/2015

https://tammymasterkey.wordpress.com/2015/03/06/week-22-harnessing-the-power-of-negativity/ 21/07/2015

http://intuitiveunderstandingmasterkey.com/tag/dmp/ 21/07/2015

http://www.backstage.com/advice-for-actors/backstage-experts/3-ways-use-fear-your-advantage/ 21/07/2015

https://www.psychologytoday.com/blog/witness/201301/the-best-predictor-future-behavior-is-past-behavior 21/07/2015

http://easym6.com/2013/06/22/some-
people-die-at-25-and-arent-buried-
until-75/ 21/07/2015

About the Book:

After years of compromising and retreating due to past, costly failures, Richard had to face the reality of dealing with the recurring challenges. In this book Richard's resolve in facing fear, whilst leveraging it, underpinned his belief that fear can only be dealt with by acknowledging fear and doing, hence "Cheat on fear".

It is my hope that in reading this book, you too will muster the courage and face fear, whatever form it may be presenting itself to you.

About the Author:

Richard Akita is the author of "Every Day in Love" and "Power of One: One Idea, One Decision, One Action". An entrepreneur and Life Performance Coach.

He loves empowering others to pursue their purpose and goals. He describes himself as "a catalyst that gets his clients from where they are to where they want to be", his role is to challenge his clients to DARE to DREAM!

ISBN: 978-9988-2-2633-6

9 789988 226336

www.ingramcontent.com/pod-product-compliance
Lightning Source LLC
Chambersburg PA
CBHW070048040426
42331CB00034B/2634